The Preacher's Prodigal Child

Dr. Bob Martin

The Preacher's Prodigal Child
Copyright © 2018
Dr. Bob Martin

ALL RIGHTS RESERVED

No portion of this publication may be reproduced, stored in any electronic system, or transmitted in any form or by any means, electronic, mechanical, photocopy, recording, or otherwise, without written permission from the author. Brief quotations may be used in literary reviews.

All Scripture quotations are taken from the King James Version of the Bible.

FOR INFORMATION CONTACT:
Dr. Bob Martin
95 Baptist Dr.
Vicksburg, MS 39180
601/618-4191
bobjoymartin@earthlink.net

ISBN: 978-0-692-15860-9

Cover Design © Morris Publishing

**Printed in the USA by
Morris Publishing®
3212 E. Hwy. 30, Kearney, NE 68847
800/650-7888, www.morrispublishing.com**

Table of Contents

Introduction — 5

Foreward — 7

Chapter One: — 9
　The Presentation of the Prodigal

Chapter Two: — 15
　The Outside Influences that Dishearten

Chapter Three: — 29
　The Effect of the Prodigal on the Parents

Chapter Four: — 39
　Seven Questions for the Parents

Chapter Five: — 53
　How to Keep them from Bing a Prodigal

Conclusion: — 62
　Can a Short Book Help?

Appendix I — 63
Appendix II — 64

Introduction:

The old preacher said "The parents of Jesus lost Him at church, and they were not the last ones to lose Him there".

I believe the tears shed for wayward children of Christian parents is probably incalculable in human terms. We will deal with the children of preachers specifically at this time, but the subject runs the gambit of parents in our churches. It can be a Deacon, Sunday school teacher, or someone in the pew or choir. It is a subject that is not talked about in "Christian circles", except in hushed tones. Parents are embarrassed by the guilt of having raised their children to be rebellious, or by what others, inside or outside their church may think of their holiness. Many times the whispering is done by church members whose children "can do no wrong", but later the terrible reality of the possession of similarity in their children rushes into their own life with a vengeance.

I first began to deal with this subject years ago because we had two prodigal children of our own. Today, there is a perception of a problem of epidemic proportions in traveling across the world, preaching and fellowshipping with Pastors and Christians. It breaks my heart that no one is dealing with the problem, but everything seems to be "swept under the table". There is a multiplicity of books and articles on the subject, many written by renowned psychologists and theologians, yet most, if not all, leave out some of the crucial questions that a pastor/Christian's family encounter with their prodigal. Our middle son and our youngest son were raised in a pastor/missionary/evangelist home. The middle son was the "elder brother" in the story of the prodigal son. He did things right, went to a Christian college, talked the good talk, but his walk was never right. The youngest son was home schooled, raised in church, served with us on the mission field, taught the Bible, prayed over, loved, and directed to the Lord Jesus as his savior. He rejected God and left home at his earliest opportunity. Joining the Army, he participated in two tours in Iraq. Along with his brother we wept and prayed over them, sought Godly counsel for them, and failed them in many ways. These are the testimonies of that life journey and the unfailing grace of God.

Please excuse the manifold usage of the first person in these writings. It is His story, but also there is a need to tell our history.

Thankfulness:

For all the books we read and absorbed.

For all the people who opened their hearts and lives to try to help us along the way, and also with the writing of this book.

For the grace of God that got us through each day.

Foreward:

Putting to paper such private and painful truths in order to offer help to so many is simply the way things must be done. While this little book contains such a wealth of spiritual insights as one of those so-called "quick reads", it leaves the reader recognizing many helpful truths and the need of a deeper and longer study of the material. It sets in order the answers of the questions of the authors. First, by learning how the Holy Scriptures apply in everyday living as individuals, and then second, by the experiences that can only come through application of the Scripture while walking and talking with God.

While employing the Bible as their guide, the authors bring help and hope from three points of view; each one with their own unique view point. It is one of the rarest reads I have seen in a long time. Unlike many modern-day writers, the authors have exposed their tragedies and triumphs, as well as the fears they overcame by faith. This they did, not to sell a book, but to present the reader tried Biblical principles that work. How so? This book incorporates three vital views approaching the subject from three positions of authority. The father as a minister and a husband; the mother as a wife and a helpmate; and the son as a father, husband and policeman. Combining their experiences they bring tremendous help to families facing the pain and embarrassment of the prodigal child; both the one in the "far country", and at the one at home! So, one may ask, "How will this book help me?"

Before I answer that question, I would first plead with you for the opportunity to give one vital piece of counsel. Set down and read Luke 15:11-32 at least 35 times. Let that reading "soak in", then read this book. This book is much like viewing the Gospels. While noting their common goal of telling the same story from different perspectives, they all bring much light to bear on the Person of Jesus Christ and His purpose. To a small degree, this is the way three people open up the painful truth concerning the prodigal and the parents. I realize, if you push this illustration too far, it will fail. But the thought of how God uses all three of these individuals to inform and minister to both the parents of the prodigal, and the children, is very unique.

Developed from the perspective of a Pastor, Missionary, Father and Husband, the writer reveals how, and what part, he had to play in the return of the prodigal. From the perspective of the Mother, helpmeet and keeper of the home, she will lend to the reader the necessity of placing themselves under the God-ordained authority in the home, while facing the pain and heart-break of struggling against her motherly instincts to recover the prodigal child. From the Son's perspective, while lending great insights to recovering the prodigal child, he brings a world of help in answering the most important of all the questions; how to keep them from becoming prodigals in the first place. I believe this book is a must read.

Pastor Greg Clemts,
Southside Baptist Church, Vicksburg, Mississippi

Chapter 1
The Presentation of the Prodigal

A 2011 Bana survey reports that "88 percent of children raised in an evangelical Christian home will leave the church by the age of eighteen. Three out of four young people leave our Baptist churches in this same age group. The some-what good news is that about half of those children find their way back.

The 1828 Webster's dictionary defines "prodigal" as "given to extravagant expenditures; lavish; wasteful; not frugal or economical; expended to excess". The Webster's Collegiate Dictionary reflects the changing definitions of words over time saying "someone who is: reckless and wasteful, someone who squanders; one who returns after an absence". There is no definite age limit given in either definition. A prodigal can be an old person, middle aged, or a teenager. They have chosen the wasteland of this world over the biblical values of their God, and the clear teaching of scripture and their elders. They are extravagant in that wasteland to spend whatever resources that come their way on the pleasures of this world, and what it has to offer. They have the values of the movie and television industry where no one has a job, no one labors, yet all have the employment of saving the world aided by an abundance of finances. The result of this kind of thinking is always a tendency to homelessness, and a debauchery of the wicked, corruption, dishonesty and depravity. Everything they work toward is the "weekend of pleasure". They have no sense of accountability toward anyone they know, especially God. Since the discipline of the home seeks to instill standards of accountability and values, it must be pushed aside, forsaken, and fled from at all costs.

My Testimony:

I was the prodigal son who raised prodigal sons. Found in a trash can one month after our birth, my sister and I were adopted into the home of Ollie and Ruth Martin. My father was a soul-winning Baptist deacon over 60 years, and my mother did about anything a deacon's wife could do in a Baptist church. It was probably DNA from my birth parents (found out later they were not nice people), and the sin nature inherited from the first father Adam, but I was adept at lying, deceiving, being sneaky, and manipulative early in life. My sinning was limited under the discipline of my parents, for which I thank God to this day. I despised my parents because of their standards, hated God for making me live in a Christian home, and sought to extract everything possible from a wicked world. At 13 years of age I raised my fist to God and demanded He leave me alone, and promised never to bother Him again. Praise His name for not answering those heathen wishes according to my request. Later that year I was sodomized by my Sunday School teacher, which only added fuel to the fire of rebellion. I started "running away from home" and getting into trouble early in life, and did so until the age of 16 years. At that time a judge looked down from his bench and pronounced "probation until the age of 21" for burglary and theft. If I got an "F" on a report card, a traffic ticket, left the state without notifying the Sheriff, I would never see the Judge's face, but they would take me directly to "Gainesville" (the Texas youth correctional facility). By my senior year in High School I was going to the bars with an altered driver's license (I already looked to be 21 years old), along with several of my friends from church on Sunday evenings after services. It was bad, and I only sought to grow more wicked and evil as I rushed headlong after sin, death, and hell.

College only made matters worse. My parole had been reversed at 18 years old for good conduct, so there was no restraint to live in a wicked manner. Having been taught to work, the available jobs were good, so college was a playground. Being away from my "do gooder" parents was a liberation I had longed for. One summer, a Baptist Student Union mission trip to Wisconsin became available, so I applied and was accepted. That summer Joy Elizabeth Whitehead entered my life, a church secretary at a neighboring church, who was later to become my wife. Upon returning home I was "kicked out" of school (a liberal Baptist university) for drunkenness, and got back home to a greeting letter from Uncle Sam. I joined the Navy that afternoon so I wouldn't have to go to Vietnam, left for Boot Camp the next morning, and two years later, got married to the love of my life. I ended up in the Arab/Israel war, spent a year in Vietnam

(God does have a sense of humor), served on an aircraft carrier and a nuclear repair ship, and left the Navy with an honorable discharge. Having no employment, the one job I knew how to perform became available, church staff (Music/Youth Director) at Hollywood Baptist Church in Memphis, Tennessee.

The problem: all this time the praying of a Godly grandmother and my parents followed me. My grandmother died just after my 12th birthday, but folks said she used to put her hand on my head and pray "Lord I pray you will save Bobby and call him to preach". There were times I came in drunk and would hear my parents praying in the night. Christians I had met later said "didn't know why, but I have been praying for you all these years". Because of this the Lord interfered, and injected Himself, into my life.

January 25th, 1971 God saved this poor, lost, rebellious, hell-bound sinner, all because people prayed, sought the face of God, and persevered before the Throne.

Preacher's children are different:

At least that's what everyone says. Oh they may not say it in words, but their expectation is much higher for the children of a preacher, because their expectations are higher for the Preacher. Many times they feel, if the preacher's children turn out bad, they have an excuse before God for their own failures. "Let's don't talk about me Lord, look at that hypocrite preacher" becomes their cry. But here's the truth of the matter, the preacher's child is the same as any child raised in church and in a Christian home. All the possibilities for sinning and for holiness, are possessed by that child.

Back in the 1960's and 70's it seemed that the devil was seeking to destroy churches by disruption among the members, and doctrinal degeneration across denominational lines. In those days of "easy believe-ism", new versions, and anti-doctrinal teachings, many joined fundamental Baptist churches to seek power and position not knowing that Satan intended to raise them up 20 years later to be the instrument to destroy churches. Next, the emphasis of satan for intended destruction seemed to be the pastor himself, by the use of men who were hirelings, who brought disrespect on every God-called pastor, and the use of women whose only goal was to destroy the called Man of God. Since the 90's, it seems that the Accuser of the Brethren has gone after the children of the preachers. Almost everywhere we turn, we encounter preachers and their wives with at least one prodigal child. Many times that prodigal will wield a detrimental influence upon the other children in the family, thus producing more prodigals.

Chapter 2
The outside influences that dishearten.

Dealing with church members:

A word of warning to every Christian parent. Just because the people around you use the title "Christian" does not mean they will treat your child in a Christ-like fashion. Many well-meaning members will use words similar to "Don't worry, you have raised them in the nurture and admonition of the Lord. You just have to trust the Word of God and His providence." Or, "they are really good kids at heart and God knows they love Him", or "everything is going to work out okay". Many times, all this verbalizing does is to drive you inward until you refuse to share any burden for the prodigal, and back up in the shadows to hurt in silence. Numerous Christians have not lived with the agony of heart, and the "not knowing where they are" of a prodigal, and simply do not know what to say. So, they parrot what they have heard from others. It is much the same at a funeral as people outside of the family endeavor to give comfort with such statements as "we are sorry for your loss" etc.

Dealing with lost people about our prodigal:

Any Godly pastor is also a witness for the Lord. In retrospect, many people in the community surrounding a church know more about the pastor than is the truth. Much gossip always surrounds the church, and especially the pastor. The Godly pastor seeks to guard his influence by guarding his moral, financial, spiritual, and family life, especially in respect to the community. When a child becomes a prodigal the community will know (if for no other reason, the company the child keeps) about the moral life, sinfulness, and character of the child. I have seen parents devastated when seeking the salvation of the lost, to be reminded of the failings of a child. "How can you preach to me when you can't take care of your own house?" becomes the cry of Satan through the lost person. All of this is designed to destroy the witness of the Man of God, the witness of the church, and the witness of the saints. Proverbs 25:26 says "A righteous man falling down before the wicked is as a troubled fountain, and a corrupt spring"; like the cows fouling up the pond with mud and feces, or a stinking, stopped up, spring. Satan always has a lost person around to watch us "mess up" on God. He also has the lost and worldly crowd around when our children mess up. Since children have no innate wisdom, but must be taught by spiritual education and experience in these matters, the situations can be devastating to the parents and the child. Of course we feel as parents that it would be good (if it were possible) to lock the child away somewhere safe until they were fully grown when they have all the wisdom of maturity. We forget that those same children learn through the experiences of life. Romans 5:3ff states "And not only so, but we glory in tribulations also; knowing that tribulation worketh patience; and patience, experience, and experience, hope; and hope maketh not ashamed because the love of God is shed abroad in our hearts by the Holy Ghost which is given unto us." Like it or not, we all have to learn the lessons of life by living through them. The Holy Ghost through the writer Luke said of our Lord, "And the child grew, and waxed strong in spirit, filled with wisdom; and the grace of God was upon him…And Jesus increased in wisdom and stature, and favor with God and man". Our children must learn these attitudes and character corresponding to the experience of the man Christ Jesus.

The other side of the coin is the accusation of our own flesh that says "lost people won't listen to you because of your own children". Of course, both are lies.

How do you deal with lost people in these situations?

Should the Man of God give up and quit his responsibility to seek the lost for Christ? Of course not. ***Please understand the reason for everything that is happening in the family of the prodigal. <u>This is extremely important to the subject</u>, because none of the rest of the book will make any sense without this understanding. Satan, the world, and the flesh desire to kill the testimony of the Man of God and remove him from the ministry. That's*** *always the final goal of the temptations, external and internal pressures, and degradation of the relationships within the family's realm of influence.* In the midst of dealing with the prodigal, we tend to lose sight of the above truth, because we tend to focus on the problem instead of the Lord Jesus Christ and the priority of obeying His Word.

Here are some of the intended goals of the wicked three (the world, the flesh, and the devil) in the life of the Preacher:

1. <u>Depression</u>. The goal of depression is to disrupt a pastor and wife's ability to reason with spiritual sound thinking, and to make them unfit to make the decisions needed to serve God. One of the problems of Post-Traumatic Stress Disorder (PTSD) among veterans, is an inability to believe the love of anyone, especially God, in the life of the person affected. Depression is one of the major symptoms of PTSD found in veterans, policemen etc. In that darkness one can doubt the love of God as well as every promise He has made to the believer. All that has to happen, is for the mind and heart of the preacher to be established upon the problem of the prodigal instead of being settled on the Lord. Once that happens, the darkness seems to envelope the preacher and the family. The associated shame (an undue and undeserved humiliation) of depression causes deep internal mortification and disgrace, which makes recovering even more difficult. One writer said, "Depression taught me to trust God in the dark

while waiting for my feelings to catch up with my faith". Sometimes that "catching up" takes longer than we can envision or imagine. In this day of "quick fixes", this one is not.

The other form of depression can be the comparison of circumstance. I know Christians who have a root of bitterness springing up in them because other Christians live in better circumstances without the pain and sorrow of a prodigal child. Many have felt this way. We have wondered if others have endured the same things we have endured. It is all too common for us to compare our experiences with others. "Why has it been harder for me than for my fellow Christians?" It is not wise to try to make certain that God's will for one person is equal to His will for another. We all have different DNA. God is the sovereign Judge, Saviour, and Educator, and He does all things well. He knows what is best for each of us. He knows what will bring the most glory to Himself. The failure to understand this concept can lead to serious spiritual problems. We have probably known Christians who have struggled with bitterness because it seemed that their problems were more severe than their friend's problems. It is not our business to make these kinds of comparisons. We are taught to accept God's will for our lives and thank Him as we appropriate His sufficient grace. Truthfully, we have no way of knowing what others are experiencing. Whatever God's will is for others, we can know that God is perfectly wise in allowing it. We can trust God while following His will for us.

2. <u>Denial</u>. One of the problems of being a pastor/preacher is that you are always dealing with people in need. That burden can become so debilitating that one can push it into the back or our mind and heart. Sometimes, the burden of the prodigal establishes itself with the same intensity, and we may not want to deal with the problem for a space of time that allows us forget the pain for just a little while. In our hearts we know it will never solve the problem, we only desire a little relief from the pain. The pain of the knowledge of the lostness and eternal damnation of a child is beyond explanation, especially when it involves a preacher's child. How do we deal with the problems, pain, debilitating pressure and fears? For a pastor to carry the load of everyone's problems is an invitation to physical, mental, and spiritual disaster. That's why it is called "burn out". 2 Peter 5:7 says "Casting **all** your care upon **Him**, for **He** careth for you" (emphasis mine). If I'm going to help my people in the midst of their problems, if I'm going to help the prodigal, I'm going to have to put them ("all" of them) in the hands of the Lord and let Him deal with them. That is more easily said than done, for it may involve a continual "casting" for days or even months or years. We dealt with our two sons over a period of 15 years. It is only the day by day grace of our loving, heavenly, Father that supplied the strength to keep on keeping on. And this was only done as we cast that care upon our Lord, and disciplined ourselves to continually and faithfully serve that same Lord in

the midst of the pain and depression. Does it mean we "back up" and never deal with the problems. Of course not. It means that we allow the Lord to live His life through us, thus allowing Him to deal with the problems while going forward in our service to Christ, and the maturing of our circumstances and experiences.

3. <u>Dependence</u>. One of the problems of this generation is that everything is equated to "fast food". When dealing with a prodigal child, the parent must understand that there are no "fast food" answers to this problem. God may save and return the child next week, but this preacher has yet to see that happen in any of the families that we have encountered. It becomes easy to depend on something other than our Heavenly Father. We become dependent on our feelings instead of His faithfulness, and the well-trained prodigal can sense that and use those things against the parent. When it happens the parent becomes the emotional victim of the abuser prodigal who seeks to keep them in subjection to their wicked wishes. They usually become their banker enabling the prodigal to fulfill their ungodly desires by financial means. Most often, the Lord is working the concept of dependence on God in the life of the parents, a lesson not soon learned. As a matter of fact, there is a lifelong lesson of patience, the dealing with a prodigal only being a chapter of the whole lesson. It also may happen that the prodigal

does not come to God during the lifetime of the parent. But whether the Lord gets them back during our lifetime or not it must not matter, and we must learn dependence on the Lord

Keeping them from hellish influences:

One of the problems with raising children is, they grow physically. Sometimes they don't grow spiritually, mentally, or emotionally in correspondence with the physical growth. Like it or not, when they reach a certain age the world tells them they are adults, whether they have the capabilities of adults or not. You can't chain them to the fireplace or handcuff them to the bed. We can make sure they are in church, send them to a Christian school, have family altar with them, teach them the Bible, and pray with them during the extent of their growing years. We can shelter them from as much of the world as possible, but the worldly influences are still around and do affect them. They do see the bill boards and hear the cursing. They have to learn to be in this world but not of this world. Sometimes all the Bible teaching and living that we do will only bring them back to center in moral living because of the constant effects of perversion and wickedness, but we keep doing it because we love the Lord and love them. Someone has well said, "the best thing any father can do for their children is let them see that he loves their mother, and the best thing any mother can do for their children is to let them see that she love, honors, and respects their father. This is especially important on the part of the father. The world is constantly teaching our children that men treat women without respect. Women are to be deceived by playing mind games with their emotions and considering them to be a piece of flesh to be used for their own pleasures. "I love you" has become another weapon to get what a man wants, instead the genuine truth of that man's character and practice. If our sons are going to learn respect for women, they have to see it modeled in a father who genuinely loves their mother. If they are going to learn respect for women, they have to be taught to respect and protect their sisters. Our daughters need to learn that a man who does not respect them will never be a good husband, and they must see that truth modeled in their father and mother. If we don't know how to deal with the influences of the world in our own lives and the lives of our family, we cannot teach our children how to deal with them also. It is not the work of the church to teach our children morals, to teach them how to love and live, or to implement that teaching in their lives. That is the specific job of the parents. The church exists to help on a community of faith basis, but first and foremost it is the work of the father and the mother. We must not just teach our children rules, but also how to establish the wisdom of the Bible as the fences and guard rails of their lives, so as to keep them out of the ditches of sin, pride and failure which exist all around them and at every turn in the road of life.

Part of that work is the establishment and implementation of the rules of the home. The rules are there to guide them, protect them, and help them establish their own discipline of a Godly life for the rest of their lifespan. If it is Bible rules, then they should never change. **Make up your bed when you get out of it in the morning** was designed to give them basic discipline. **Turn the lights off when you come out of a room** taught them (and us) that members of the church gave sacrificially so we could have lights and also that we should be accountable for God's money. **If you see someone who needs help, help them,** was another rule that was designed to enable them to understand they were not the center of the universe. The children used to laugh at us because I was trying to help Joy and she was trying to help me at the same time, and basically all we were doing was getting in each other's way. Another one of the rules of our home was, and is, that **everybody in the family knew the location of everybody else in the family**. That rule hasn't changed because all the children left home. Joy and I still abide by that rule. Joy and I tried to **never argue in front of our children, and never make a decision about them in front of them.** We went to the discussion room (our bedroom) and then returned to give them our decision. If one of them wanted to do something and requested it of me the answer was always *"have you asked your mother and what did she say"*. That was the same answer the child got from their mother. We did not want the child dividing the parents to "get their own way". Practical things that help a peaceful home are a necessity. ***If someone says "I'm sorry" they have humbled themselves to apologize and you <u>always</u> accept the apology with grace.*** The failure to accept an apology brought instant wrath without apology from the nearest parent. ***Church came before family and family came before school. Everybody sat down for the supper meal.*** If there was a late practice at school, then supper waited until they all were there. ***Yes sir, yes ma'am, please, thank you.*** Simple things that help them function in life.

Ephesians 6:4 says "And, ye fathers, provoke not your children to wrath: but bring them up in the nurture and admonition of the Lord". Looking back on the lives of our children, I do not see that family rules or discipline provoked my children to wrath, but the application of those rules without fairness or love did provoke them. It is difficult for a child to live according to family rules if they do not know or understand those rules. I've had to go back and apologize for expecting more out of my children than the Lord expects out of me, for demanding perfection when I am incapable of performing perfection myself.

How do we deal with temptation in the life of the child? <u>My son can help here</u>:

How Can I Help My Children With Temptation?

Proverbs 1:10 says "My son if sinners entice thee, consent thou not."

I don't draw a distinction here, and I don't think Solomon was drawing a distinction either, about the origin of the enticement. Saying 'no' here is universal, regardless of the origin of the temptation.

Just as Solomon did, when you help you children deal with temptation, you must plan ahead. That was why he wrote it. We sometimes miss the planning nature of our God. He likes a good plan. A good plan starts with "intel". Intel in the military is actionable information. If we have good "intel", we can use it to make good decisions.

<u>First</u>, teach your children to be wary. Teach them that God loves people, but trust is applied to people and situations through Christ. He is to direct our trust. So when sinners approach us, they must be seen through the truth of God's direction, His Word.

<u>Second</u>, teach your children that they are the ones who have the choice. God gave them the choice. They are not being pulled past the point of that choice. That is a great gift He has given to all of us. We get to choose. Your children might feel swept away by the moment, but God always provides an escape so that we can bear it. He made that promise; I Corinthians 10:13. In that passage Paul is dealing with many different types of sin; idolatry, fornication, drunkenness, murmuring etc. No

matter what the temptation, we still get to choose.
<u>Third</u>, teach your children that God empowers His promises. I would like to drill down here much further, but the fourth point is so important in relation to the third and I don't want to diminish it.
<u>Fourth</u>, teach them that His power is not freely given. His grace is free, but not His power. We can't live how we please, and expect the Creator of all things to empower our unfaithful decisions. We must be in tune with His Plan found in His Word. God likes a good plan, right? He does, but a good plan is His plan.

Chapter 3
The effect of the Prodigal on parents

The breaking of the father's heart

What every prodigal fails to understand is – the concept and implementation of "tough love" is much harder on the parent than it is on the prodigal. The self-inflicted guilt that consumes the Man of God is terrible. Sometimes, in the night hours, the reminder of our conscience, and the accusations of the Accuser, become almost unbearable, reducing us to tears and sleeplessness. I know the scripture is out of context, but it certainly is applicable – "weeping may endure for a night, but joy cometh in the morning" is a certain truth for the parents of the prodigal. Sometimes it is a joy just to see the daylight, and yet, there may be the fear of another night without sleep. One scripture passage that sustained my heart was the story of the Prodigal Son. That father never stopped loving the son, and never stopped looking down the road for the son. I believe his faith in God was the sustaining part of both loving and looking.

One of the problems in dealing with a prodigal is in the area of oppression and temptation timing. When the constants of these two areas moves into a lengthy amount of time, the parent tends to see it as normal. We began to look toward a day when the pain will end, the praise will reinstate as normal, and the problem will be solved. In dealing with a constant sense of spiritual harassment, we tend to set the praise of the Lord and the enjoyment of grace "on the back burner". The problem becomes paramount and the enjoyment of the Lord is secondary. There must be a definite desire and work to set things in proper order or the oppression of depression, denial, and dependence will take over the life of the father of the prodigal.

In the midst of a breaking heart there must be a stability in discipline on the part of the father. The applicable scriptures are demanding and complete. To fail to discipline the child means a lack of love on the part of the parent (Proverbs 13:24). If we are not careful, the application of discipline will become an action of anger over what the child is doing to the family and themselves. This discipline must not become personal, but must be done in the "admonition of the Lord" (Ephesians 6:4).

Mama's heart and love is different

For the father of the prodigal, it sometimes feels that he is fighting for his child and yet, having to fight his wife at the same time. We do not understand the loving heart of a mother because, as a man we live by reason, and her heart does not "make sense" to us. Therefore, this section will be written from a mother's heart (my wife's heart), <u>addressing those issues</u>.

From the first day of birth, the baby you have in

your arms is one that depends on you to care for them. Such an awesome responsibility. God gave you a human being to keep for Him.

A mother's heart loves and gives in spite of the actions of the child. We will at times discipline them when they go past the boundaries that are set for them. But, for some reason we will go that extra mile to get them back into line by forgiving them, and giving them another chance. To our determent, we sometimes let them go too far. Whereas a father's love is different. They look more to the future and what the child will become if they are not disciplined as well as loved. Sometimes the father has to give corporal punishment to bring them back to the boundaries set for them. It is because they love the child that they will take time to correct the problem, praying and hoping the child will turn. I remember times I would have to go into another room when my husband had to discipline our children, but I knew it was for their good, and I did not need to interfere. That would have been detrimental to our children. If they thought they could get me to side with them and get them out of trouble, they would never had learned their lesson. It is always stressful to the relationship of a husband and wife when she sides with the child. It will destroy the authority of the father, and tear the relationship apart.

We raised two prodigal sons. We took them to church, prayed together, had devotions together, and yet, when they reached adulthood they left home and decided to go their own way. They supposed they were enjoying the "freedom" of no restraints, doing their own thing. Mom and Dad prayed for them often, and asked God to bring them to Himself. It is a difficult thing for a mother to give her child up to someone else, even though it involves giving them to God. I was afraid of what God might have to interject into their lives to bring them to Himself. But, one day I realized, that was the only way for our children to finally come to the end of themselves and turn to Christ.

One son had to suffer through losing his health (he had cancer twice), and lost his job because of that health. He almost became homeless, but, by the grace of God he finally came to the end of himself and asked Jesus Christ into his heart. The best way to describe my feelings during the course of time he experienced all of this, is to describe a mother with a sick child. Mentally and emotionally you suffer watching that child, knowing that there is absolutely nothing you can do to help, but pray. You weep over them because you love them. You want so much to comfort them and ease their pain, but you can't because of the sickness. You desperately wish to push them into salvation so their life is changed, want to help them however you can, and at the same know that only God can melt the heart of stone and turn their face heavenward. What a joy and relief to see our son come to Christ, to love us again, and desire to be around us again. We give God the glory for all he has done.

The second child was a religious prodigal (the

Elder Brother in the story of the Prodigal Son), that in reality, did not know Christ in his heart. He says he had "head knowledge, but not the heart knowledge". It is wonderful to know that God can move in your child's heart when they are physically so far away, when even because of a false profession, you may not know the need. Again, we have given thanks, and thank the Lord today, for the salvation of our sons, and for the many people who prayed and offered up supplication to our Father on their behalf.

The despair of not knowing:

One of the worst parts of the parent's relationship with the prodigal is the heart-break of "not knowing". Where are they? Are they dead or alive? Are they well, or is their health gone? Have they dived headlong into the cesspool of drugs, alcohol, prostitution, the sodomite culture, or any other of the myriad of sinfulness in this wicked world? It is a series of questions that plague the parent of the prodigal. It is even worse for the parents of a daughter prodigal because of the dangers involved to women alone in this wicked world subject to the desires and deceptions of wicked men. These depressing questions are not designed to engender hope or dependence on God, but to create havoc in the emotional and spiritual life of the individual. That havoc is in turn designed to lead to a mental or physical breakdown. The trichotomy of the world, the flesh, and the devil attack the child of God with this tactic to separate them from faith and dependence on God.

This will cause a parent to cry themselves to sleep at night, and at other times lead to sleepless nights. Just the phone ringing causes a fear and cringing. There is a tremendous load of guilt and condemnation that beats us up on a regular basis. "Why did God even let me become a parent when He knew I would be a failure"? As one writer said "Every mistake I had ever made replayed in my mind like a spinning tire in a muddy rut". Prayer becomes a replay of the situation instead of a cry for help. The heavens "become brass" and God doesn't seem to be listening. Sometimes we cry "God don't you care?" We decide to "give up", and yet we cannot. One mother said she came to the place she told God "I'm over it, God. They can do whatever they want to. I can't live like this. I'm not praying anymore!" Of course, that only lasted for a few minutes and then the concern returned.

For the believer, a knowledge of the Word of God can mean even more despair. For example, one of the problems in knowing and believing the "whosoever will" of the Bible is recognizing the "whosoever won't" of the lost individuals in the world who fully and completely reject God's Word and love. The fear that the child will never repent, never trust Christ, never know peace, and end up in the Lake of Fire for eternity is almost debilitating to the parent.

The problem with all of this is that our relationship with the Lord slips. We become controlled by, and almost addicted to, worry and concern for the prodigal, and our relationship with the Lord begins to suffer from neglect. Our prayer life becomes a "rehash" of the events of life, the mess the child is in, the failures of discipline and the blaming of God because the Bible verses did not work, and our inability to "fix" the problem. If we are not careful, our daily walk with the Lord, the time spent in the Scriptures, and our witnessing of the grace of God to the lost, takes a back seat to our concern over the prodigal. Church worship becomes a constant "prayer request" for the prodigal. All we speak of unto other Christians is our pain and distress over the prodigal. Our life becomes controlled with the agony of the prodigal sliding off into hell for an infinity of time. We are not controlled by the Holy Spirit but are controlled by the prodigal, which many times, is exactly what that prodigal child desires, and works toward. If the prodigal child can control the situation, the parent, and the finances of the family, they have everything they desire in life.

The decision of faith:

So what do you do if you do everything right? One of the main problems of being a parent is that we have to perform one of the most important jobs in the world without even a miniscule bit of experience to draw upon. It is like moving from Kindergarten graduation to the job of CEO at Boeing Aircraft in one day. Do everything right? Oh please! Like that's going to happen when both a parent and a child with a sin nature are involved. The real question is, where do I go to get real help? From a lost person with a worldly philosophy? Not hardly. From the psychologists, the psychiatrists, the reformers of this present evil world? You must be kidding! And yet, I know parents who have raised their children as close to right as anyone we know, and still they had a child that went off the "deep end". I learned years ago running construction crews and a deck crew on a towboat that you don't waste time placing blame. Don't allow the situation to get worse while you are looking for the guilty party, and chastising people about what they did wrong. **Instead, I need to fix the problem!** We are eaten up with guilt; always considering how bad our child turned out, worry in buckets full, and all the time the problem of a prodigal is not being remedied or even close to being fixed. Actually, it is being ignored. Don't fall into the trap of playing "the blame game". Satan loves to waste your time and kill your witness by causing you to live and function in that spiritual and emotional snare.

At this point I always think of the new mother who was told by her friends that "those old women don't know anything about babies, just get the best books and the best advice from the best experts, and it will be okay". Even though she was a Christian, she ignored the advice of scripture which says "That the aged women likewise… that they may teach the young women to be sober, to love their husbands, to love their children…" (Titus 2:3-4). Finally, out of complete frustration and physical weakness (26 hours without sleep will do that to a new mother), she called her mother and found out that most of the experts needed to take a back seat to the one who had already raised four children.

Where do you go for help? There are people who have been through the process of the prodigal, and they may be of help to you. Others are going through the process of the prodigal themselves and are good to vent with and cry with. The best place for help is still the Lord and His Word. That brings us to the real place for help.

Chapter 4
Seven Questions for the Parents of a Prodigal:

Here are seven questions we had to deal with in asking God to help us with a prodigal child. They are not easy questions for any parent to answer, especially for the parent who is a saved, blood-washed, born-again child of God.

1. **Do I know how to hear from God?**

Many Christians **do not** know how to get "cleaned up" spiritually and get to the place in prayer where they can hear from God. It usually takes a time of prayer and fasting, asking and listening, and seeking the face of God and the answer from God. Sadly, this has become almost nonexistent among Christians, Baptists, and even some preachers. It is not a "run into the presence of the Lord for a while" deal. It is not even the "faithful" saying of a prayer each day for years. We had dealt with our son for 15 years, but it wasn't until 14 years and 9 months of that time that we heard from God. That session of prayer ended in an assurance of the salvation of that wayward, lost boy. It was three months later before he was saved (his oldest brother led him to the Lord), but we knew the victory had already been won before that day on our knees. The experience taught me much about the presence and power of God I had forgotten from past years. I knew how to pray for lost people, but did not know that it was different for my children. I knew how to enter the warfare for the souls of lost men and women, but then it became personal, when it was my son, the intensity of the war exploded. One famous evangelist said that he was saved because his mother stated "Go on to the night club, but I am getting down on my knees and seeking God until you get saved." He came home and went to bed with his mother on her knees crying out to God, but by the following morning, he was on his knees beside the bed crying out to God to save his wretched soul.

There are three ways that God speaks to His children. First, and foremost, is His Word. Second, He speaks by the Holy Ghost, through faith, to the heart of the Child of God. And third, by the counsel of other Christians and the circumstances of life. Of course, the third one is the least dependable of the three because the terrible three (world, flesh, and the Devil), love to get involved in our circumstances. In dealing with the second work (the voice of God), there is an assurance given in answer to prayer that is as certain as life itself. A mother was told by the officials from the prison where her son was incarcerated that the son had died in a prison riot. Her reply was that "there was a mistake in the accounting of the prisoners, because God had assured her that He was going to save the boy before she died and he had not yet been saved". Try as they could those officials could not get her to accept the death of the son. The next day the mistake and the boy were found, and less than a year later he was led to the foot of the Cross and the Lord by a prison chaplain. When the parent hears from God, the faith (convincing work of the Holy Spirit) given the parent to trust the Lord is a fact already settled in the courts of God, and the heart of the Child of God.

Joy and I remember the confidence of the Lord after His assurance to save our son. For my wife it became a battle between feeling and faith (well, me also, but not as much, ha, ha). She said, "Many times I feel he isn't going to get saved before I die, but it doesn't matter if I go on to Glory, I still know the Lord is going to save him". It is that Bible "hope" (confident expectation) that gets you through the situations, and sometimes the day, especially when things get worse before they get better. It was three months later that Jason got saved, and it seemed that all of Hell was turned loose to expel its fury and filth against us during that time, and every encounter with him was an anger explosion and hurling of unreasonable insults. But, we could deal with him in love and grace because the battle had already been won, and we knew what he did not know, but would come to know when he got saved.

2. Do I know how to get right with God?

Being right with God is not a once-a-year revival meeting, cry some tears and have a good time, item. Our Lord is interested in a daily "walk" rather than a Sunday morning conviction and altar call. How did I get saved? By repentance (lost people don't go to hell to pay for their sins, they go to hell because they won't come out of their sins) and <u>faith</u>. How do I live for the Lord? Colossians 2:6 says "As ye have therefore received Christ Jesus the Lord, so walk ye in him". Again, how did I get saved? By repentance and faith. So how am I to live the Christian life? By repentance and faith. The Bible says "repentance toward God and faith toward the Lord Jesus Christ". My sin is against God the Father, and He is the Heavenly Father who deals with rebellion in my life. My walking faith is toward the Lord (notice the order of the words) who is first the ruler (Lord) of my life and then my savior (Jesus) and my sustaining High Priest (Christ). How do I get right with God? First confess my sins to the Father and then cast all my being on the Lord to allow Him to rule and reign in my life. Someone will say "I did all that when I got saved". Actually walking through this life is a daily thing and not a one-time event. Sometimes it seems that I am repenting and casting myself on the Lord sixty times in sixty minutes. Sometimes it is an all-day event of separating myself from food and people with intense prayer. Four decades ago this was called "keeping a short sin list" by many Baptists. It means we stay close to the Lord so He can call our sins immediately to mind by the Holy Ghost of God, with the result that we can get those sins immediately confessed and forsaken. The intention of this practice is habitual, not just intermittent. Have I reached that level of perfect sanctification yet? Of course not, but surely we can keep on the path to stay as right with the Lord as possible, even with the temptations and trials, and pressures of this present life, and especially when they become exacerbated with stressful circumstances.

3. Is the child saved or lost?

The tendency is, to believe the child is saved because of an outward "profession", growing up in church, or comparing them to all the "bad" young'uns around. So often, the "profession" of the parent is not good, and the parent transfers their own salvation experience to the child. Then they want to make excuses for the behavior of the children because the parent is following a defective Christian value system of their own.

We always want to believe the best for our children, especially the heart of the mother. Vance Havner wrote many years ago:

Gibbon describes the degeneration of Christianity under the Greek scholars of the 10th century, who handled the literature and spoke the language of the spiritual, but knew not the life; 'They held in their lifeless hands the riches of their fathers without inheriting the spirit which had created and imparted that sacred patrimony. They read; they praised; they compiled; but their languid souls seemed alike incapable of thought and action.'

The Pharisees of Jesus' day handled the things of God, read the Scriptures, faithfully kept the letter of the law, were painstakingly separated from sins. But the publicans and harlots went into the Kingdom before them.

To have grown up in a Christian home and in a church, early fluent in the speech of the Kingdom, familiar with its subjects and observing its practices, yet never a citizen, produces a type of sinner often harder to awaken than the most ignorant heathen. Truth long heard and not acted upon means awful self-deception (James 1:22). Second generations do not inherit salvation. God has no grandchildren."

It has been interesting to note, that in all the reading on the subject of prodigal children, only one author ever deals with salvation in the child, and that in a very limited and religiously liberal way. All the writers seem to desire a change in the outward life of the prodigal from drugs, alcohol, sexual sin, rebellion etc., but do not understand that inward salvation brings the change that turns that prodigal from these outward sins to Christ.

Was the prodigal son in Luke 15:11-24 saved? Modern theology and liberal Biblical interpretation says he was probably saved and just left home to "sow his wild oats". This theology says we can never get doctrine from a parable. But honestly, we can get Bible truth and principle from any of the parables. After having rebelled against Godly love and discipline, he "headed out" and spent all his inheritance in the "far country". After spending it all, enduring the famine, and becoming employed with the degrading and demeaning job of "feeding swine", the Bible says "he came to himself". At this point his mind was changed, his attitude was changed, his emotion was changed, and his will was changed. He repented. He even had the right "reasoning" which brought the ability to charge himself with sin, recognize his own unfitness of all the blessings of the father, and he left the pig sty for the father's house. The key to the parable is "And he arose, and came to his father" turning his back on the "far country". As one author says, "he could not get to the father without leaving the "far country" of sin and rebellion. His repentance and faith changed "what he loved, how he purposed to live, and where he desired to be located". He did not come bargaining with the father, asserting his demands of the father, or dwelling in his rebellion against the father.

Interesting also is the fact that the elder prodigal never got saved. A prodigal can remain at home. Millions of prodigals do remain home in these present days because of the recognition that things are much better financially in the father's house. An outward display of obedience ("neither transgressed I at any time thy commandment") can belie a heart of absolute rebellion covered by a hypocritical disposition. This parable was not enunciated for the common sinful people, but for the Pharisees and Scribes in attendance. A prodigal can remain in the house, practicing a small degree of rebellion and disdain for the parents, smoking their dope, fornicating in the shadows, making fun of the things of God, sucking down the finances of the parents, enjoying the technology of sin, and quoting just enough scripture to qualify as somewhat spiritual, while making everyone miserable with an unloving and profane spirit. Whenever judgment gets to close, they get spiritual again. But here's the real questions -

1. Has the child ever known real Holy Spirit conviction of sin (John 16:7-11)?
2. Was there the blessing of scriptural peace when they got saved (Romans 5:1)?
3. Was there the change of life, attitude, and concern for the lost, that comes with salvation? Or, did they just put on the robes of the hypocrite they had viewed in others as they practiced their "religion of pretense"? So often this is not an informed pretense. Because the child has never really gotten lost (been under real Holy Spirit conviction), they never repent and they rely on an experience they had early in life. I asked a pianist at church, "Please tell me about your salvation experience?" Her reply was "I have been saved since the age of four, so I don't remember the experience. You will have to ask my mother; she's the one who told me about my getting saved." Having seen that scenario played out in Baptist churches for years, my heart goes out to those who are doing the best they can, but have no foundation of salvation. Too often the child is led through a prayer, taught the foundational values of morality, hard work, church attendance, and Bible reading, but never have seen themselves as a vile, wretched, sinner deserving hell and needing the salvation of the Cross. Because I was so good at lying, I was able to fool my father (a soul-winning

Baptist deacon), and numerous pastors and preachers until the age of twenty seven. The other side of the subject is this: I met a dear lady that received salvation when she was four years old. She knew she was a sinner, didn't want to go to hell, and asked the Lord in child-like faith to save her. She has lived twenty six years as a saved person. Has she always done exactly what was right? No! But it is not in her saved nature to fornicate, smoke dope, get drunk, and cuss. Why? Because at four years old her life was changed. That's the difference.

Until we get an "answer from God" on this question of salvation, we don't really know how to pray for the child. Someone will say "well no one can know if another person is saved". Well, God knows, and He can tell His child so that His child can pray effectively for their sons and daughters.

4. If they are lost – is it a problem with demon possession?

This is a tough one to face and evaluate. Are they enamored with the demonic worlds of Goth, satanic worship, violence and witchcraft, video games and movies, full of depression, suicidal, have a hatred for God and the church, have a hatred for a Godly parent, try to find comfort in the world, drugs, alcohol?

After salvation our son said "I always loved you-all, I just didn't like you, or want to be around you". Do they become angry, take an attitude of rebellion, get quiet or get away when you talk about the Lord or spiritual things. If they have this problem they need deliverance before there can be salvation.

The Canaanite woman in Matthew 15:21-28 had the problem of a demon possessed daughter. She came to the Lord desperately, and would not be denied the help she was so badly needed. She was ignored, called a dog and not worthy to be helped in her situation by our Lord. She was willing to accept the fact that she had no standing before God and was, in truth a wicked sinner from a wicked place, if the Lord would simply deliver her daughter from possession by a demon. But, she was also a woman of faith who believed that the only person who could deliver her daughter was the Lord Jesus Christ. Are you willing to come to that place also in your spiritual life? Whatever obstacles are placed in your path, you are going to get to the Lord for help?

5. **Do you believe they can get saved on your faith?**

Luke 5:20 says that the man sick of the palsy got saved on the faith of his four friends. He got saved on their faith! "And when He saw their faith, he said unto him, Man, thy sins are forgiven thee." God can do the same for our children as well. **If we ask the Lord to save them, have we been convinced by the Holy Spirit that** they are lost, that they need salvation through the Cross of Jesus Christ, and that God will do it? Faith is a work of the Holy Spirit (John 16:8 – "reprove" means to convince), so we understand the Holy Spirit has to convince us of sin, righteousness, and judgement (that we are headed to hell). That convincing work is called "faith". Saving faith is the gift of God (Ephesians 2:8), so why is not abiding faith, living faith, everyday faith, praying faith, believing faith, also a gift of God? I have been convinced that I am saved, am saved for eternity, am going to heaven, that the Bible is the Word of God (King James Bible), that the church is always a local entity, that salvation is by grace, and on and on. If God the Holy Spirit can convince me of those things, can't He convince me of the salvation of my children? Sin is always unbelief, period. I want my way, doing my thing, my way. Through faith I accept the Lord's way and by His grace trust Him for the outcome.

Usually our problem as a parent is the problem of convenience. We are so busy in our normal life we don't take the time to get alone with God, or we get forgetful of the things of God. Most of the time a prodigal is the product of a build-up of neglect – how much time do we spend daily praying for our children, seeking answers about their salvation and walk with the Lord? If we are inconsistent in this area, our prayer life becomes a time of alarm and running to God in panic.

Let me say here, many times we never really pray for a child until they do become a prodigal. The cares and problems of this life have a way of taking the time we should be praying. Looking back, I realize that this kind of prayer for all my children should have been my norm, all their lives.

6. **Are you willing to place them totally in the hands of God?**

Wow, talk about tough! Here's where the "rubber meets the road", the real place of reality, truth in its purest expression. The answer to this question is much more difficult for mothers. Mothers in their 40's tell me that one of the worst times in their lives is seeing a son or daughter leave home to get married, complete their education, or join the armed forces. The reason being that she has been involved with "fixing them" all their lives. But now she knows the child is going to "mess up" to a certain extent, yet she is unable to fix any problem they may have. Did she do enough, teach them enough, help them enough, love them enough? Why can't she go visit them in Boot Camp or at their college dorm every week to help them? Why can't she be the one who trains the new daughter-in-law or son-in-law? It's tough! The placing them in God's hands is not a one-time giving them up to God. One problem both fathers and mothers have with placing the prodigal in God's hands is that you will find it a continual process over a period of time. But, there must come a point in time when the child is handed over to the Lord for Him to deal with the child according to His will. My father said that he came to that place when he turned me over to the Lord, knowing that things were going to get worse before they got better, but also knowing that as long as he kept "bailing me out of trouble" the Lord would allow him to do so, and the Lord could not deal directly with me. I was in jail awaiting trial. The pastor and my mother came into the cell and visited for a few minutes but my father was not with them. I was my same old smart-alecky self, and then a few minutes later Dad came into the cell. He said "You got yourself into a mess of trouble this time son. To which I replied 'yes sir'. Well, I guess you are just going to have to get yourself out", and then he walked out and closed the cell door behind him. Looking back, I know it was one of the hardest things he ever did in his life. But it was a turning point in my life, and I know he left that cell broken hearted. This is the toughest part of the whole process.

A good passage of scripture is in 1 Kings 17 where Elijah is sent to Zerephath to be fed by the widow woman. This was the home ground of Jezebel, her father being the ruler of all of Zidon. Even though the Lord hid Elijah in plain sight among the relatives of Jezebel, He was already working on the other end of the situation. That widow woman was not a believer in the Lord God because she said "the Lord thy God", referring to Elijah (17:12). But she was also at the end of her rope getting ready to bake a biscuit and die of starvation. She was ready to grab at any straw to save her and her son, but there was only one straw – Elijah and his God. Many times God has to do that to us; getting us to the place where we will take our hands off the situation and let God work, but He won't work until we do take our hands off the situation. He has to bring us to the place of need, reliance, dependency and faith, forcing us to be governed by Him, depend on Him, and walk by faith in Him through the situation. It also means we don't do lip service and expect help, we are ready to do the work of dependency – "and she went and did..." (17:15). The Bible puts it this way, coming to the place where we are "casting all your care on Him, for He careth for you" (1 Peter 5:7).

7. **Are you willing to get alone with God until He gives the answer?**

This means individually as well as together. Many times God will drive us to Himself as we pray for our children. But, we must set aside time to a season of prayer and seeking God's face, even if means in our bed throughout the night. We have to learn "planned determination", the art of setting aside time and learning patience to stay with the Lord until He answers. So many Christians think because the request is made, there is nothing more to do and no more time to be spent before the Throne of God. We have taken the verse of song (Take your burdens to the Lord and leave them there) to mean, just dump them in the Lord's lap and run on back to whatever we were doing. We must learn to pray until we hear from God that He is going to intervene and interfere in the life of the child. If you are saved, that is exactly what our Lord did in your life to bring you to salvation.

Chapter 5

How Do You Keep Them From Becoming A Prodigal?

This section is written by our son who deals with prodigal, rebellious children on a daily basis, and has great insight into the problem.

First off, I'm not a PhD, a certified counselor, or even an academic. I can only say that my qualifications to put pen to paper, so to speak, are my sons. We judge qualifications by pieces of paper. We should judge them by people. My 18-year-old hugs me before bed and when he leaves in the morning. My 16-year-old tells me about how his day went, with more than an, "it went ok." My 13-year-old likes to listen to 80's pop music and road trip songs with my lovely wife. If I am stipulating the following principles, and having sons that hate me and hate God, it would be like being a fat, fitness trainer. The principles of proper diet and fitness might be true, but you don't know that from looking at the trainer, because he says what is right, but he doesn't do what I right.

Second, there are three rules you need to know about your children. These rules don't originate into existence when the kiddos are born, but always, repeat **ALWAYS**, spring into existence after they are born. Of course, each child is different. I was twelve years old when the rules happened to me. One of my sons was four years old, so smarter than me I guess. Most children will probably develop these rules right about the time they start puberty.

The rules are as follows:
1. <u>I know I exist</u>. The child begins to understand that they have free-will. Often, they grasp very early on, that they can tell Dad and Mom "no." You must be prepared for this. You have to understand ahead of time the reason for this response, and have a plan for how to respond. By the way, "Because I said so" isn't the right plan. I took the time to explain to my sons that authority is a mantle, given by God, to help the child grow in the right direction. You, the parent, stand in the place of God for your children. Therefore, you will answer to God for how you raised them. Therefore, your children should obey because God loves them and you love them enough to direct their lives in a positive manner. The kiddos will fidget real hard here, but if you have already laid a good foundation on trust in God, understanding (as much as humans can) who God is, his principles and his nature, they will be much more likely to obey. You, as well, will find yourself empowered to direct and use that authority correctly because you have acknowledged God to them.
2. <u>I don't like myself</u>. Makeup, new clothes, new friends, new technologies, etc. are often the trappings of a child who sees the dark inside themselves. Your children are much less likely to run to the world's false promises if they feel secure in their relationship with you. You **should not** attempt to become their friend. You are not their buddy or their friend until they are grown, you are the parent. <u>But</u>, you must absolutely listen with full

attention, when they want to talk to you, and then thoughtfully respond. Your responses must instruct your children in God's Word. I often find myself recounting Bible stories to my sons when they come to me with a problem or a situation. I have found that recounting God's Word within the context of their daily struggles helps them to remember it better. This is a simple association exercise, to associate God's principle with their problem through His Word. By the way, it means I have to learn the Word of God to be able to use the Word of God to help my children. I know this elicits a "duh" response from many parents, but it is a truth that must be worked out in our everyday lives by reading, learning, memorizing, and studying the Word of God.

3. <u>You can't tell me what to do</u>. "Rebellion". No other word fits. Let's be honest, we weren't looking for God or His interference. Therefore, we want what we want and nobody better stand in our way. Your kids aren't any different. Funny thing is, if you have spent time working on rule number one and two, rule number three gets smoothed out. Rules one and two are the setup to the real problem, rule number three. If you have a plan already in action, you can work through the rebellion problem, and work through it with your relationship with both God and your children intact.

In short, the child assumes the human condition. If you look closely, every ungodly thing a person does is the result of those rules. We all realize that we are sinners, but for the child, these rules represent the first time that they understand the rules for themselves, and in themselves. To see if I'm wrong, take a little time and go to a public place. Any public place will do, just as long as there are people, especially children. Think about these rules as you see people move and interact. Look how they dress. Observe the way they seek approval or attention. The rules fit all people. Teenagers are the most conspicuous. A gaggle of teenagers will talk about other people, disparage each other, seek higher social standing, etc., all because they realize that, their existence is a dark, hollow place. The dark in that place is a thing, not the absence of it, because it is sin. They know it, but not in conscious reality. In the part of the mind that reacts to horrifying sights by fleeing or cowering or pretending to not notice, they know. Few adults, and even fewer children, realize or can articulate the presence of the sin nature. So they treat themselves and others like trash to distract away from that most awful part of what they are, sinners. The idea is to make everyone look someplace else, or at someone else, so they won't see the real me.

I know, I got pretty dark there and the truth can be hard to handle. Notice how I didn't spend any space dealing with how terrible they are? Wouldn't you agree that, because we are all sinners, there really isn't any need? We are all terrible! Besides, that's not the design of this chapter. That lovely gem is what follows.

So here we go. Below I've listed seven principles

that I (attempt to) follow with my sons.

Patience- When you try to relate a principle of Godly living to them, they won't understand what you mean now, but they will remember it later. I have a tendency to pontificate. I admit it. I don't have a problem with it, but you should see my son's eyes go blank after a few minutes. I know that in Deuteronomy God said to discuss the Law with our children while we walk in the way. He didn't say beat it into them or scream it at them. In fact, the command is barely even contextual because it means to do it before the problem arises. You see, you have to plan and speak before your child messes up. God did that for us in His Word. He did it because He loves us. What if we didn't know the stopping point and kept walking over it? Thanks to His Word, we do know the stopping point. It follows then, that we need to discuss God's Word, laws, precepts, and principles, early on with our children. Proverbs chapter five is a great example. Here Solomon tells his son, you are going to meet temptation in this world. It will be in the form of a lost woman who is seductive, will endeavor to talk you into sinning with her (her *"lips...drop as an honeycomb, and her mouth is smoother than oil"*), but in the end you will lose everything. Her goal is your wealth and she doesn't care what she has to do or how she has to do it to obtain her end desire (Proverbs 11:22). So, wait on God and find the wife of His choosing and learn to love her.

I know that you most likely can point to numerous

examples of what following God's Word have done to bring you His peace, and also what disobedience has cost (What God hates – Proverbs 6:16-19; What adultery will do to you – Proverbs 6:26-35; etc.). Yeah, you gotta include the bad stuff too. Which brings me to the next point.

"Do as I say, not as I do" is a recipe for disaster. I'll be really quick on this point. At some point you will tell your children to do something (or not to do something), and they will reply in so many words, "You did that once, so you are such a hypocrite!" Your response will depend on whether or not you are actually a hypocrite. Back in the 80's there was a commercial that shows a dad confronting his son about the young man's drug use. The concerned father asks, 'How did you learn to use drugs?' The fellow screams at his dad, "From you, alright! I learned from you!' The moral being, get your house in order before confronting you children. By the way, if you are harboring sin, don't expect the Holy Spirit to bless your parent/child interactions. Hint, hint…

So that was what happens if you DO happen to hypocrite. I'm going to go out on a limb here and assume that most parents used to do things they see the kiddos doing, but you the adult are not presently doing. Therefore, you are not a hypocrite, but you are experienced in the matter at hand. That's the reason you understand the behavior of the child. Don't forget here, that the issue is the child's behavior, not your history. If you used to partake in the sin about which you are correcting your child, this is a great opportunity to gain emotional ground with them. Admit it (see rule 4). Tell the young one that you, in fact, did do those things. Then tell them that those things hurt you and almost destroyed your relationship with your family. Most importantly remind them that it hurts their relationship with God. God loves them and wants to keep a good relationship with them. He goes just as far as He can in His relationship with them, but they have to reach out as well. For our Lord, it was His sacrifice on the cross for our sins. For the child, it is obedience. Ok, ok, I wasn't that quick, but I hope that you can forgive me and move forward to point three.

Actions Speak (scream) Louder than Words- They won't remember what you say as much as how you say it in the actions of everyday life. Remember, you are the adult and they are just now realizing that they exist.

'I'm sorry' might not fix everything, but it fixes most things. Wow! As an adult we attempt to avoid this one don't we?

If you want your children to grow up, start growing them up. Children want to please their parents. No, really, they want to make you happy. As an extreme example, in West Memphis, Arkansas, a sixteen-year-old boy shot two police officers because he thought it would make his dad happy. Sadly, it did make that particular father happy. I won't get any deeper into the weeds of that story, but the concept remains. Children adopt OUR morality first. If you point to God, they will start looking at Him. If you make the problem about them, or about you, they will look at you.

You aren't the authority, you are just the messenger. Maybe you don't have to remind them of this, but you certainly need to remind yourself of this. You wear a cape, or rather, a mantle. It is a mantle of responsibility. God gave it to you, and He expects you to wear it well.

You don't have the strength or wisdom, or patience, or anything else, to complete this job, but God does. In fact, He gives you particular gifts to get the job done. I call it "fix it and find it." In a more politically correct sense, it would be called "critical thinking skills." God gives you the ability to work through problems, to fix stuff and to find stuff. How many times has a son or daughter called down to you crying out in utter anguish, "Dad (I'm a dad, so we'll go with that), I can't find ____!" You then make the effort to go upstairs and, after a minute or less, find that exact thing. You then give the "Is this really my kid?" look, toss it to them, and go back to watching television or whatever. I hate to tell you this, but that's God's gift to you, not your gift to yourself. You have a great many gifts to use in His service. Don't be a Samson, who liked to use God's gifts for his own desires.

What Do I do when I Do Everything (including prayer) and They Still Reject God and Die Without Christ?

One of the Bible problems is everyone has the ability to reject God. We call it "free will" which means that every human being has the God-given ability to say "no" to God. This is the worst fear of every born-again Christian parent. The Bible says that Cain "went out from the presence of the Lord, and dwelt in the land of Nod". Nod means vagrancy or wandering. He became a vagrant wanderer. We pray that our homes are a place of the presence of God, and sometimes that is the rub. When a Cain doesn't want to be around the presence of God, they naturally become a vagrant and leave home to wander. Isaac and Sarah wept and cried over the choices of their oldest son Esau. He even tried to perform careful repentance with bitter tears and, as far as we know, never got to God (Hebrews 12:15-17). There are other instances in The Book, of people who rejected God and never got saved, and every one of these people had a mother and a father. Spurgeon's mother told him that if he rejected Christ and salvation she would witness against him at the Great White Throne judgment as to his knowledge of the Bible and salvation. It is a terrible reality that every Christian parent has to face.

How does a Christian parent face the rejection of God, along with the rejection of the parent?

1. Let go of the past. God's not so concerned as to where you have been, as to where you are going

Do we quit living for the Lord? Do we quit witnessing for the Lord? No, and of course not. The Apostle Paul said "forgetting those things that are behind, and reaching forth unto those things which are before, I press toward the mark for the prize of the high calling of God in Christ Jesus" (Philippians 3:13-14).

2. Learn anew how to walk by faith. We forget that we "can do nothing" without our Lord. It is all of Him, by Him, about Him, concerning Him, and with Him.

Conclusion:

Can a short book cover the situation of every prodigal and the parents? No, that won't work, will it? Some children go crazy at an early age and others go crazy after they leave home. Some are quiet in their rebellion and others are loud and stubborn. Some will walk away and others are confrontational. Because they all have different DNA, because everyone in the world is different, they all act different. But here is the truth - only the Lord can conquer their hearts, whatever their intelligence, disposition, or attitude. Somewhere we must come to the conclusion that "our help is in the Lord", and that help can come from nowhere else. When we understand that fact, we can cast the child, and ourselves, upon the Lord.

Appendix One

How To Get Back Up When I Get Down

1. Focus on Christ.
2. Rise up – encourage yourself
3. Get sinless – or as close as you can!
4. Witness about God's grace (salvation), goodness, glory, greatness. "A witness a day will keep the doubting away" and will cause great dependence on God. It will also cause a seeking of personal righteousness, and a sense of the presence of God (Romans 1:1).

Appendix Two

WEEKLY EXERCISE - "Knowing God in Purity"

1. Allow God to teach me about purity in my life:
    1) To give me a desire for holiness.
    2) To give me a hatred of sin.
    3) To give me a desire to do right in every relationship of life.
2. Allow the Holy Spirit to set high standards of honesty and kindness.
3. Allow the Holy Spirit to set personal standards of conduct and morals by the
    Word of God.
4. To make friends with Godly people.
5. To become accountable to the Lord for my life and for my sins.
6. To ask myself "what do I need to do in accordance with the Word of God" in
    every situation of life.